D0546423

INTERPRETATION

Discovering the
Bible for yourself

WILLOW
CREEK
RESOURCES

JUDSON POLING
BILL DONAHUE, SERIES EDITOR

ivp

InterVarsity Press
Downers Grove, Illinois
Leicester, England

InterVarsity Press
P.O. Box 1400, Downers Grove, IL 60515, USA
World Wide Web: www.ivpress.com
E-mail: mail@ivpress.com

Inter-Varsity Press, England
38 De Montfort Street, Leicester LE1 7GP, England

InterVarsity Press®, U.S.A., is the book-publishing division of InterVarsity Christian Fellowship/USA®, a student movement active on campus at hundreds of universities, colleges and schools of nursing in the United States of America, and a member movement of the International Fellowship of Evangelical Students. For information about local and regional activities, write Public Relations Dept., InterVarsity Christian Fellowship/USA, 6400 Schroeder Rd., P.O. Box 7895, Madison, WI 53707-7895.

Inter-Varsity Press, England, is the book-publishing division of the Universities and Colleges Christian Fellowship (formerly the Inter-Varsity Fellowship), a student movement linking Christian Unions in universities and colleges throughout the United Kingdom and the Republic of Ireland, and a member movement of the International Fellowship of Evangelical Students. For information about local and national activities write to UCCF, 38 De Montfort Street, Leicester LE1 7GP.

All Scripture quotations, unless otherwise indicated, are taken from the Holy Bible, New International Version®. NIV®. *Copyright ©1973, 1978, 1984 by International Bible Society. Used by permission of Zondervan Publishing House. Distributed in the U.K. by permission of Hodder and Stoughton Ltd. All rights reserved. "NIV" is a registered trademark of International Bible Society. UK trademark number 1448790.*

Cover design: Grey Matter Group

Photo image: Boden/Ledingham/Masterfile

Chapter icons: Roberta Polfus

USA ISBN 0-8308-2065-5

UK ISBN 0-85111-529-2

Printed in the United States of America ∞

19	18	17	16	15	14	13	12	11	10	9	8	7	6	5	4	3	2	1
15	14	13	12	11	10	09	08	07	06	05	04	03	02	01	00			

Contents

Introduction

Some time ago, Russ Robinson (director of small group ministries at Willow Creek Community Church and concept editor on these guides) and I were talking about how to help groups get a firm grip on the Word of God. Both of us had studied and taught courses on the Bible, but what about small groups? What if we could put something together that could be studied as a group and yet have much of the information people would normally find in a class or course? Well, hats off to Russ, who came up with the idea for Bible 101 and cast the vision for what it could look like. Soon we were outlining the books and the result is what you have before you. So welcome to the Bible 101 adventure, a place where truth meets life!

Traditionally the subject matter in this series has been reserved for classroom teaching or personal study. Both are places where this curriculum could be used. But this work is primarily targeted at small groups, places where men and women, old and young, rich and poor gather together in community to engage fully with the truth of God's Word. These little communities can be transforming in ways that classrooms and personal study cannot.

Few things in life are more fulfilling than drawing out the deep truths of Scripture and then seeing them at work to change a life into the image of Christ. Getting a firm grip on the Bible and its teachings is paramount to a mature and intelligent walk with God. We are to worship him with all our heart, soul, mind and strength. And the Word of God is central to accomplishing God's desire that we be fully devoted to him.

The team from Willow Creek—staff and volunteers alike—has labored diligently to provide you with a group-friendly process for understanding the Bible. Kathy Dice, Gerry Mathisen, Judson Poling, Michael Redding and I have worked to provide something that merges content and process, learning and application. Now it is up to you to work together to discover the riches that lie ahead for those willing to do some work and take a few risks. But we know you are more than ready for that challenge!

To make these studies more productive, here are a few suggestions and guidelines to help you along the way. Read carefully so that you get the most out of this series.

Purpose

This series is designed to ground a Christ-follower in the study and under-standing of Scripture. It is not designed for someone who became a Christian last week, though sections of it would certainly be good. And it is not as rigorous as a Bible college class or seminary course might be. Bible 101 means *foundational,* but not easy or light. So be prepared for some challenge and some stretching. This may be the first time you are exposed to certain theological concepts or terms, or to some more in-depth methods of Bible study. Celebrate the challenge and strive to do your best. Peter tells us to "make every effort" to add knowledge to our faith. It will take some effort, but I can guarantee it will be well worth it!

Prayer

When approaching the Word of God, you will need to keep a submissive and teachable attitude. The Holy Spirit is eager to teach you, but you must be willing to receive knowledge, encouragement, correction and challenge. One educator has taught that all learning is the result of failed expectations. We hope that in some ways you are ambushed by the truth and stumble upon new and unfamiliar territory that startles you into new ways of thinking about God and relating to him through Christ.

Practice

Each session has the same format, except (in some cases) the last session. For five meetings you will learn skills, discuss material and readings, work together as a team, and discover God's truths in fresh and meaningful ways. The sixth session will be an opportunity to put all you have learned into practice. Studies are designed as follows.

Establishing Base Camp (5-10 minutes). A question or icebreaker to focus the meeting.

 Mapping the Trail (5-10 minutes). An overview of where we are headed.

 Beginning the Ascent (30 minutes). The main portion of the discussion time.

Gaining a Foothold (3 minutes). Information to read that identifies core issues and ideas to keep you on track with the journey.

 Trailmarkers (10 minutes). Important Scriptures for memorization or reflection.

 Teamwork (15 minutes). A group activity (sometimes done in subgroups) to build community and share understanding of what was learned.

 Reaching the Summit (5 minutes). A chance to summarize and look back at what has been learned or accomplished.

Close in Prayer (as long as you want!). An opportunity to pray for one another and ask God to deepen the truths of Scripture in you.

You can take some shortcuts or take longer as the group decides, but strive to stay on schedule for a 75- to 90-minute meeting, including prayer time. You will also want to save time to attend to personal needs. This will vary by group and can also be accomplished in personal relationships you develop between meetings.

Preparation
Preparation? There is none! Well, almost none. For some sessions reading ahead will be suggested to provide an overview. But the sessions are designed to be worked through together. We find this builds a sense of team

and community, and is also more fun! And there is something about "discovery in the moment" rather than merely discussing what everyone has already discovered outside the meeting that provides a sense of adventure.

We wish you the best as you draw truth from the Word of God for personal transformation, group growth and kingdom impact!

Bill Donahue, Series Editor
Vice President, Small Group Ministries
Willow Creek Association

Session 1

Principles of Interpretation

Understanding the need for and practice of good interpretation skills.

Establishing Base Camp

When I started taking an interest in the girl who eventually became my wife, I decided I needed to explain my growing feelings. I stopped-by late on a weeknight and took her to a nearby coffee shop. After some surface-level chit-chat, I looked over the coffee mug at her and said, "Deb, I've come to the conclusion that you are dangerous material." The phrase "dangerous material" sort of popped into my mind, describing both my delight and mild fear that we were becoming close.

She looked down coyly, raised her eyes and said, "Well, I think *you're* dangerous material!"

Wow! She liked me too! I knew that she had understood me, and we were headed in the same direction emotionally.

Was I wrong! Later I found out that when I told her she was "dangerous material," Deb didn't have a clue what I meant. She guessed I must have been feeling the need to put distance between us—that she was dangerous material I was intending to avoid, not dangerous material I wanted to get to know better! So to play it safe, she just repeated back to me what I said. She hoped that way—whatever I had meant—her feigned agreement would cause the least problems.

Fortunately, within a few days we cleared up this glitch in understanding, and we've gone beyond being dangerous to being married. But this experience illustrates how communication is only effective when both parties understand each other. Whether it's in a marriage, a work of literature, a business setting or even the Bible, if we don't understand what the other person meant, our interpretation is going to be flawed.

✓ Describe an experience when someone misunderstood your

directions. (The results could be comical or disastrous.) Why is it especially frustrating when we are not understood?

Mapping the Trail

✓ What are some truths you believe that you are sure come from a correct interpretation of the Bible?

✓ What gives you confidence about your interpretation?

✓ In your experience, when you come across something in the Bible that confuses you, how do you try to get at the true meaning?

Beginning the Ascent

God's Word comes to us as words on a page. If you think about it, he could have chosen a variety of means to communicate. He could have used an audible voice and waited until we invented tape recorders to speak to us. He could have made a special device that when you touch it, you instantly know his thoughts. He could have directly inscribed words on a rock, such as when he wrote the original Ten Commandments (Exodus 32:16; 34:1). But God instead gave us a book. It took hundreds of years to complete, using many different human authors who each used different personal and literary styles. The Bible contains history, poetry, letters, genealogies, visions, direct prophecies, songs, checklists, quotations from other authors (sometimes even pagans!), collections of wise sayings, richly symbolic language and strikingly plain instructions. It is tempting, in the face of such diversity, to throw our hands up and say, "Why didn't God make it *simple?*"

✓ What do you think are the advantages in God's use of so many people, so much time and such diverse literary types to record his full message to humanity?

✓ In the face of such a rich tapestry of communication, how do we get at God's message? Are there special means we must use to understand what God is saying? Do we need special "glasses" that will show us what he really meant, or do we have to go to seminary and be trained in the original languages before we can make sense of the Bible?

Thankfully, the answer to all these questions is no. Though portions of the Bible are harder to understand than others, the central truths of Scripture are clear. They are stated in a variety of ways and repeated often so we will have clarity.

The first rule of thumb is to read the Bible as you would any other book or newspaper. The Bible was not written in some kind of code. It is written in plain language. The Greek and Hebrew of the original texts were the common languages of day-to-day business and correspondence.

Gaining a Foothold

The golden rule of interpretation is *What did the original author mean for the original audience?*

Original Author: Imagine reading a newspaper article and telling the author that although he wrote, "The referendum passed by a large margin," you interpreted his words to mean the referendum didn't succeed because a large margin of voters "passed" on casting their votes. That's not what he meant; that's also not what happened. But if you insist on your "interpretation," you are doing so against the author's intention. That's the sign of a bad interpretation (not to mention your interpretation doesn't match objective facts!).

Original Audience: Now imagine reading a newspaper from one hundred years ago. In an article the author writes, "Any man of the house who doesn't have a stockpile of wood or coal during the cold months of winter is foolish." Those were the fuels for heating and cooking in a home at the time. Now looking at your situation today, you know you don't have a stockpile of wood or coal. Do you conclude the author is saying *you* are foolish? At the end of the nineteenth century, not providing fuel to heat one's home was foolish. But in this day of gas and electric heat, wood and coal aren't necessary. So you are not foolish for not stockpiling such fuels, even though it was true for the original audience. Once you understand that the core issue isn't wood or coal but *provision,* you can make the application to your own situation—make sure your gas bill is paid so your local utility company keeps servicing you! You may in fact be the "woman of the house"; but the message interpreted this way makes sense both in its original context and when applying its truth to modern life.

With any Bible passage ask, "How would the author explain himself if cross-examined?" That is the interpretation you're after.

Let's expand a bit on the above golden rule. R. C. Sproul suggests these three simple rules for accurate interpretation:
1. Interpret the part by the whole.
   * Scripture interprets Scripture so the whole remains consistent.
   * The clear interprets the unclear.
   * The primary interprets the secondary.
   * That which is stated multiple times interprets that which is said only

once or rarely.

2. Follow the literal sense.

• Attempt to go with the obvious meaning rather than some "hidden" message.

    • Simple sense is better than contrived.

    • Follow the rules of the type of literature the passage belongs to. Don't force poetry to follow the rules of narrative or apocalyptic material to follow the rules of historic material and so on.

3. Use the grammatico-historical method.

    • The grammar and historic setting of the passage dictates its meaning.

    • Elaborate or multilevel interpretive schemes are suspect.

✓ Do you agree with the above points? Would you want to add or subtract anything from the list? Why?

> "What kind of a God would reveal his love and redemption in terms so technical and concepts so profound that only an elite corps of professional scholars could understand them? . . . At the same time, there is enough profundity contained in Scripture to keep the most astute and erudite scholars busily engaged in their theological inquiries for a lifetime." (R. C. Sproul, *Knowing Scripture*)

Trailmarkers

Read 1 Corinthians 1:26–27. What kinds of people did Paul write to?

✓ Assuming this letter is also inspired by God, what corollary can you make about the diversity of people God expects to read his written revelation?

✓ Read 2 Peter 3:15–16. Here, Peter writes that the apostle Paul's letters contain "some things that are hard to understand." (Isn't it a comfort to know someone as close to Jesus as the apostle Peter at times had trouble understanding Paul?). What word or phrase does Peter use to describe what people do with these teachings?

✓ How does that differ from proper rules for handling Scripture?

Teamwork

During the Middle Ages, church officials thought that only the clergy should read the Bible. Those leaders believed that if every Christian had a Bible, they would probably come up with erroneous interpretations because they lacked the proper training and spiritual qualifications. Furthermore, it would lead to divisions in the church because people would challenge official church teaching as a result of their fanciful interpretations.

> "To check unbridled spirits [this Council] decrees that no one ... presume to interpret [the Scriptures] contrary to that sense which the Holy Mother Church, to whom it belongs to judge of their true sense and interpretation, has held or holds." (The Council of Trent, 1546)

Other Christian leaders, especially the during the Reformation, tried to make the point that people should have the Bible in their own language regardless of the possibility for misinterpretation. Their belief was that common people could understand the central truths of the Scriptures. Wide distribution of Scripture was a safeguard against wrong views because the increase in study and discussion would lead to better understanding. To them, the Bible was not a confusing mystery only to be interpreted by a religious elite but a book written for all humankind. Misinterpretations may occur. But how much better to have the Word available for people to read so it could keep doing its work.

Divide into two teams. One team will represent a religious establishment trying to protect the masses from possible misinterpretations. The other will represent church leaders who believe each person should be able to read and interpret the Bible for him- or herself. Take a few minutes for each team to compile as many reasons as possible for their views. Then stage a mock debate with each side presenting and countering the other team's points. You don't have a lot of time, so get your arguments together quickly and jump right into the debate. Have fun!

"Unto a Christian man, there can be nothing either more necessary or more profitable than the knowledge of Holy Scripture. . . . These books, therefore, ought to be much in our hands, in our eyes, in our ears, in our mouths, but most of all in our hearts . . . [the Bible is a book for all to] read, mark, learn, and inwardly digest." (The Anglican Church Formularies)

The Clerical Elite *Why Only Duly Ordained Leaders* *Should Interpret the Bible*	**The Reformers** *Why Everyone Should Read* *the Bible for Themselves*

After the debate, summarize the main reasons for each position in the chart above.

Reaching the Summit

Imagine you're having a conversation with a friend about a particular passage. Your friend says, "Well, what that verse says to me is _____." Based on things you've discussed in this lesson, how can you help your friend deal more objectively with the Scriptures?

What the Bible says...	Exegesis	Leading the meaning out of the text
What the Bible means...	Synthesis	Putting the message together with all the Bible's teachings
What the Bible tells me to do...	Application	Obeying rather than just hearing the Word

Next Session

Think of some examples in which people from another culture might misunderstand you or you don't understand them. If you have traveled and actually experienced such a misunderstanding, come prepared to share it.

Close in Prayer

Focus on thanking God for giving us his Word in its rich and multifaceted form. Thank him that the central truths—his eternal being, his endless love, his holy nature and the way of salvation through Christ—are abundantly clear and understandable. Pray for humility to let the Word say to us what God intended it to say instead of what we might distort it to say.

Session 2

Context & Culture

Finding the original context of a passage.

Establishing Base Camp

The professor gave a stirring lecture. The students at this prestigious seminary came from all over the world. They sat spellbound, captivated by his vivid description of the details surrounding Jesus' crucifixion. The professor not only painted a picture that everyone could see and relate to, but brilliantly illuminated the rich spiritual significance of that event. On the cross, he had said, it looked like Jesus was defeated. Satan was the apparent winner, having destroyed the Son of God and ended his ministry. Yet an invisible transaction had taken place that made salvation possible. When Jesus died, he had paid the price for our sin, so his death became our ransom. Then three days later when Jesus arose from the grave, the tables were completely turned. The professor concluded, "Now it was God who was the winner, and Satan was left holding the bag."

The class dismissed with a fuller appreciation for what Christ had done for humankind. With one exception—a student from a Near Eastern country. After all the other students left, he meekly approached the teacher. "Doctor" he asked, "What was in that bag?"

By not being familiar with the American expression, this student misunderstood an important part of the lecture. The same can happen when we read the Bible. By not knowing the original author's intent, culture or audience, we can miss parts of his message to them—and therefore misunderstand its application to us today.

✔ Describe a crosscultural experience where communication was difficult for you (or for the person you were trying to communicate with). What factors do you think can help make a crosscultural message more understandable?

Mapping the Trail

✓ Some people say, "If the Bible is God's Word, then it applies equally to us as it did to people back then." What qualifications, if any, would you add to this statement?

✓ Some people say, "Because the Bible was written in a specific culture and time, it has little relevance today." What qualifications, if any, would you add to this statement?

✓ Other people say, "We don't need to know all the scholarly information about the background to the Bible; the Holy Spirit will lead us to the correct meaning." What qualifications, if any, would you add to this statement?

Beginning the Ascent

✓ Consider the following headline: "Bears Maul Lions." If you saw this at the top of the sports page, what would it mean?

✓ Now picture reading the same headline above a picture in *National Geographic.* What would it most likely mean in that context?

✓ Consider yet another situation: the monthly Cub Scout newsletter describing a recent holiday-wreath-sale competition. What would it signify there?

In each of the three examples, the meaning of the words is dramatically influenced by the context. The perspective of the author and the setting of the phrase make for three different messages. Furthermore, you cannot get at the meaning simply by grammar alone. Looking up the words in a dictionary or knowing the "original Greek" of this phrase is not much help.

The Bible often contains teaching that is easy to misunderstand if we don't first grasp the culture and context of the message. While the different interpretations might not be as drastically different as the above examples, knowing the use of words or phrases in a culture and in the context of the original message is always an aid to understanding.

The Bull's-Eye of Context and Culture

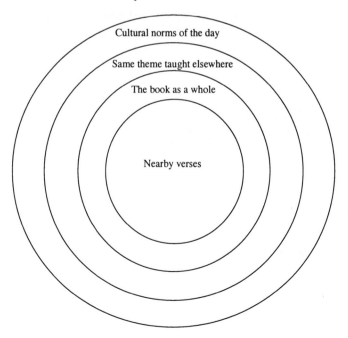

Cultural norms of the day

Same theme taught elsewhere

The book as a whole

Nearby verses

Here are some examples of Scripture where each of these come in to play.

Nearby verses. 1 Corinthians 8:5 says, "There are many gods and many lords." The Jehovah's Witnesses use this verse to support their view that Jesus and the Father are two separate gods (Father = God and Jesus = a god), thus undermining the Trinity.

✓ Read all of verses 5 and 6. What does the context show is really the case?

The book as a whole. Philippians 2:12 says, "Work out your salvation with fear and trembling." Does Paul think the Christian life is full of misery and uncertainty? Does he think we have to earn our own salvation? The book of Philippians is probably the most joyful book in the New Testament. Paul uses the words *joy* and *rejoice* over and over (skim it for yourself and see). That context alone tells us he doesn't view the Christian life as misery.

✓ What additional light does the next verse (Philippians 2:13) shed on the topic of who does the work of saving us?

✓ Now read Philippians 3:3-9. How do these verses square with a "pull yourself up by your own bootstraps" view of salvation?

✓ What is a better way to explain Paul's teaching?

The same theme taught elsewhere. Consider again Philippians 2:12.

✓ How can comparing Philippians 2:12 with Ephesians 2:8-10 help us see the relationship between faith and works in Paul's theology?

Cultural norms of the day. Galatians 5:1 says, "Mark my words! I, Paul, tell you that if you let yourself be circumcised, Christ will be of no value to you at all."

In Paul's day, circumcision was an exclusively religious practice. Some people from a Jewish background who became Christians thought it should be continued as a rite of religious initiation for all males. Their insistence on this practice called into question what they were actually trusting in—the cleansing of Christ's forgiveness or that outward sign of the old covenant. Men from a non-Jewish background who chose to follow Christ but then got circumcised "to play it safe" were in effect saying, "Christ's work is good, but not enough—I need Christ *and* this." Such a practice exposes their lack of understanding what salvation is all about. It must be "Christ plus nothing," or the Christian gospel is no gospel at all but another religious system designed to obey your way into God's favor.

✓ How would you put into your own words what Paul is saying to men of that culture?

✓ What would be his admonishment to men in our day based on the timeless truth imbedded in his culture-specific statement?

Here are some biblical examples of statements that were not interpreted correctly in their original context.

✓ *Example one.* In John 2:19–22, how did the Jews misunderstand Jesus' words? (Note this misunderstanding resurfaces at Jesus' trial in Mark 14:55–59.) Imagine yourself back in that scene, watching that heated exchange: what factors besides Jesus' symbolic language do you suppose contributed to their inability to grasp his message?

"In Bible study we start as flies on the wall, watching God deal with people of the past, overhearing his words to them and theirs to him, noting the outcome of their faithful or faithless living. But then we realize that the God whom we were watching is watching us, that we too are wholly in his hand and that we are no less called and claimed by him than were the Bible characters. . . . Having seen what the text meant for its writer and first readers, we now see what it means for us." (J. I. Packer, *Truth & Power*)

✓ *Example two.* Paul also had his words twisted. Read Romans 3:7–8. What is the essence of their slander? Based on what you know about Paul, what statements or truths was Paul probably presenting which these slanders then distorted? (See Romans 3:21–24 and 4:5–8 if you need help.)

Trailmarkers
✓ 2 Timothy 2:15 is a great summary of the kind of care we should take with God's Word. What does Paul tell Timothy to do?

✓ What words does he use to describe the person who does this?

Teamwork
✓ Think back to New Testament times (the first century A.D.). As a group, come up with a list of as many customs or cultural practices you know of that are different in our day.

First Century Culture and Customs

✓ How would knowing more about these help your understanding of the Bible?

✓ What tension do you feel about trying to sort out what is cultural and what is timeless in the Bible's message? (It's okay to admit this is sometimes hard.)

Reaching the Summit

It has been said you can prove anything from the Bible—if you take
statements out of context. A hostile

reader can say the Bible makes ridiculous claims by failing
to grasp the true intention of the author. But most of us are not antagonistic
about the Bible, we just want to be sure we've correctly understood what it
says and the implication of that teaching for our own lives. To do that we
must pay attention to the lessons learned in this chapter about understanding context and culture.

Now below, fill in from memory "The Bull's-Eye of Context and Culture" from earlier in this lesson.

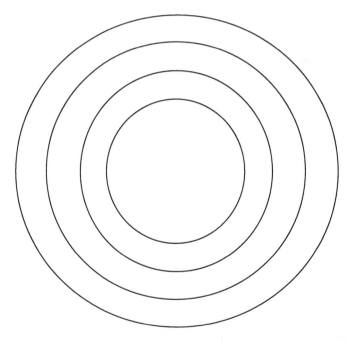

✓ Based on things discussed in this session, what one or two
tips stand out for you that will help you in your study of the Bible?

Next Session

Take a look through your bookshelves. How many different types of literature are represented? Come next week with a list of these.

Close in Prayer

Thank God for giving us his Word and for giving us tools to help get at the truths expressed there. Ask him for help in doing the work necessary to accurately interpret the things written in Scripture. Thank him that although at times this requires some effort on our part, the amazing thing is how much we can readily understand.

Session 3

Discovering the Meaning

Learning inductive Bible study methods which help us to interpret Scripture.

 ### Establishing Base Camp

My first year of college I got to know a group of Christians who had a ministry on campus. Many of the members lived together in two houses just off campus—one for the men and one for the women. I periodically went to their Sunday services and some other activities they sponsored. I admired their dedication to Christ, and the rich community they experienced with each other was something I had only dreamed about.

In their zeal to develop young Christians into leaders, they eventually adopted a teaching that all the men in the fellowship should aspire to leadership roles—specifically, to become elders. They claimed to have biblical warrant for this belief. They quoted 1 Timothy 3:1, "If any man sets his heart on being an overseer, he desires a noble task." *Who among us shouldn't desire something the apostle Paul calls noble?* they reasoned. Most important, the church needed leaders, so by using this verse to stir men into developing their leadership abilities, the church would meet a pressing need.

Problems developed, however. Many men simply weren't cut out to be elders. The Bible teaches that we all have different spiritual gifts, so to assume that every male member of the group would automatically be a good elder flew in the face of the Bible's direction to serve according to giftedness, not gender. Men who felt uncomfortable with this call were seen as weak or unspiritual. Instead of being encouraged to grow and serve in harmony with their pattern of giftedness, some men were being shoe-horned into training and expectations that didn't fit who God made them to be. At the same time women were not being encouraged to use their God-given gifts.

Now it was true that because of the emphasis, many more leaders rose to the surface than would have otherwise. But at what cost? Bottom line: the Bible says, "*If any man* sets his heart," and they distorted it as "*Let every man* set his heart."

✓ Do you think it's rigid to make a big deal about a minor misinterpretation of the Bible when motives are sincere and good still comes from it? Explain.

✓ Why do you think God doesn't always immediately "unbless" a person or group who adopts an erroneous teaching?

 Mapping the Trail

✓ What types of literature do you have around your house? What do you like about each type?

✓ When a husband wants to tell his wife he loves her, he can simply say, "I love you," or he can take a more creative approach such as writing a poem or story that illustrates his affection. What are the advantages of each approach? What are the limitations of each?

✔ When children are little, parent's instructions have to be very plain; as they get older, good communication becomes more diverse and multifaceted. What parallels can you make between these stages of the parent-child relationship and how God communicates to us through the Bible?

Beginning the Ascent

Reinterpreting the Bible: In some circles it is considered a worthy goal to reinterpret a document according to the whim of the reader. Coming up with "original" interpretations shows creativity, which is supposed to be a good thing.

Reinterpretations may also be considered a valuable technique to keep old, out-of-date documents "living" and relevant. Sometimes our legal system uses this method to take antiquated laws and keep them applicable without the bother of having to write new legislation.

> "As soon as the reader's outlook is permitted to determine what a text means, we have ... quite possibly as many meanings as readers." (E. D. Hirsch Jr., *Validity in Interpretation*)

This practice is called *eisegesis,* reading meanings into documents, which is the opposite of exegesis, the careful study of the original meaning of a text, getting at the truth that the original author would endorse.

A big problem exists with such a methodology when applied to the Bible. Setting aside the author's intention sets the reader up as a superior authority. In that case the text isn't instructing us, but we readers are telling the text what is true. Not only is that position arrogant, it is dishonest because it doesn't let the Bible speak for itself. Who among us would want to write instructions and then have them set aside by the very people we're instructing? What if we left a will, only to have it "reinterpreted" in such a way that our actual wishes were revoked—all in the name of supposedly helping our words have greater relevance after we're gone?

Gaining a Foothold

Exegesis: To lead the meaning out from the text
Eisegesis: To push a meaning into the text

Sometimes the tension of interpreting the Bible is stated as two opposing sides: on the one hand, there are those who take the Bible "literally," and on the other hand, those who don't. (Those who don't, allow for figurative or metaphorical interpretations.) But that is a false dichotomy. The real distinction is between those who practice exegesis and those who practice eisogesis.

For example, when the Bible says the land of Canaan was "flowing with milk and honey," the most conservative Bible interpreter wouldn't suggest the people had sticky, milk-coated feet from the mess they had to walk around in! It is a poetic description that when correctly interpreted yields the meaning the original author intended—the land was abundantly fruitful. This interpretation takes the Bible "literally" because it interprets the phrase according to the type of "literature" (note the correlation *literal, literature*) to which that phrase belongs (a metaphor). For someone to suggest the literal meaning of the original text was "a sticky ooze permeated the ground" is to practice eisogesis—all in the name of being literal.

✓ What are some "literal" truths in the Bible that are taught in nonliteral phraseology?

The issue becomes more controversial when, for example, historic events are interpreted as nonhistorical teaching tools. Consider the central miraculous claim in the New Testament: the resurrection of Jesus. The authors of the Gospels explain the resurrection as a historical event that actually took place. Yet some modern interpreters suggest there was no physical resurrection, but rather the resurrection descriptions are an elaborate metaphor for how the teachings of Jesus begun to "live again" even though the man Jesus had died. If the original authors of the Gospels meant this, then that would be the correct interpretation of their writings. But if they meant the corpse of Jesus somehow changed into a glorified being—contiguous with the man Jesus yet somehow spiritual and new—then the modern interpretation fails on two counts. First, it is not an accurate description of the original authors' meaning. Second, it isn't the truth about what actually happened back then. It would be eisogesis and a distortion of truth.

✔ Why do you think some people want to force historical events to have only allegorical or metaphorical meanings?

If you come to the Bible with the belief that miracles are impossible, then you must remove all miraculous events, or at least reduce them to parables or metaphors. But that pre-intent (which flows out of your bias, not the Bible) destroys the original view of the authors, who clearly did believe miracles had taken place in their presence (and most of them staked their lives on it). Better to recognize the Bible often records amazing events that the authors fully endorsed as real and historical. Now the decision is up to you—not to reinterpret the Bible to suit your antisupernatural presuppositions but to surrender to its claims and allow it to reform your skeptical heart.

Types of Literature in the Bible

Once we accept that we must always let the Bible speak for itself, we still have to interpret it. The difference is that we're not using interpretation as an excuse to be "original"; we're using all the tools available to us to get the message that is really there in the text, put there by the original author. Because the various authors used various styles and literary devices, we must pay careful attention to those differing genres.

Some Common Types of Literature in the Bible

Type of Literature	Description
Narrative or history	A recounting of an actual event or a long series of events.
Didactic	Any book or part of a book that is directly teaching its readers to believe or do something.
Parable	A made-up story which attempts to teach a lesson.
Proverb	A wise saying that helps one in practical, day-to-day living.
Psalm	A song; poetic reflections coming from a wide range of emotional states, sometimes extolling, other times crying out to God.
Poetry	Employs colorful, often visual language and a variety of figures of speech to communicate truth. The Hebrew style of poetry most often takes the form of parallelism, the rhyming of ideas (rather than how words sound) for emphasis.
Epistle	A letter written from a Christian leader to a person, a local church or a group of people.
Apocalyptic	A highly symbolic story describing cosmic struggles and God's eventual triumph over evil.
Prophecy	Writing as if God is speaking directly, containing rebukes, comfort and sometimes (but not always) predictions.

One of the most common mistakes earnest Bible students make is to take *narrative* texts and automatically assume they're *normative*. Thank God the Bible is accurate and tells us what people did; that doesn't always mean it's telling us what we should do. Many stories tell us about sins to avoid, not behavior we should copy.

Along similar lines, events in historical texts often show us God's power and thus straighten our faith. But clearly, signs such as Moses turning the Nile into blood or Jesus walking on the water are not intended as "daily events" (They weren't so at the time, nor should they be now.) That is not to say miracles don't happen today. It's just that we must carefully distinguish between what the Bible *describes* and what it *prescribes*.

Narrative texts are not necessarily *normative*.

Descriptive texts are not necessarily *prescriptive*.

What is *generally* true is not *invariably* true.

Another common mistake is to take license with poetic texts. We need not be put off by so many time-less truths that are taught using poetic language—as if we can't trust the Bible's integrity because it doesn't say everything in a crisp, unambiguous way. Similarly, when the Bible gives a proverbial saying, by definition such a statement is only generally true, not absolutely so. "Look before you leap" is great advice and so is "He who hesitates is lost." Neither is a cosmic absolute, and biblical proverbs likewise must be handled carefully. (Proverbs 26:4 says that you shouldn't "answer a fool according to his folly" and 26:5 says, "Answer a fool according to his folly".)

✓ What help do you need to handle these different types of literature more effectively?

✓ Look at the chart "Common Figures of Speech in the Bible" on the next two pages. Does using so many figures of speech imply the Bible is not accurate? Explain your answer.

Common Figures of Speech in the Bible

Name	Characteristic	Examples
Phenomenological language	Describes events as they appear from the point of view of the observer; not scientific but still meaningful.	"The sun came up at 6:30 a.m." "They spread out to the ends of the earth."
Simile	Two things are compared using a word such as *like* or *as*.	"God's love is like a sunny day." "She was beautiful as an angel to me."
Metaphor/Analogy	A word or phrase usually used to designate one thing is used to designate another; a comparison.	"That fox King Herod." "A sea of troubles." "God is light."
Anthropomorphism	Descriptions of God that use human characteristics to depict some action or aspect of his being.	"God's mighty arm held back the evil." "God came down to see for himself."
Round numbers	Estimates of time, people and size.	"They were enslaved for 400 years." "5000 people gathered."
Compressed events	Omission of detail not essential to the point of the story.	"In Matthew 9, Jairus says his daughter is dead; in Mark 5 and Luke 8, he first says she is sick, and then receives word of her death."
Hyperbole	Exaggeration used for vividness and impact.	"All of Jerusalem went out to see him." "If your hand causes you to sin, cut it off."

Metonymy	Using a word but meaning something related to it rather than it's common definition.	"She was a bad seed" (*seed* means child here). "He loves violence" (*love* means "has a propensity toward"). Crucified on the tree (*tree* meaning "the cross").
Type	A reinterpretation of a thing or event showing a deeper, more abiding significance.	Abraham's sacrifice of Isaac prefiguring Jesus' death on the cross. The rejection of Hagar/Ishmael illustrating the need to reject bondage to the OT Law.
Paraphrase	Use of approximate wording which captures the essence but is not verbatim.	All four Gospels have slightly different wording for the sign above Jesus' cross.
Idiom	A way of saying something peculiar to a group of people.	Three days and three nights (a unit of time which includes any part of three consecutive days). Adam knew his wife (had sex with her). Children of Israel (the whole adult nation).

Trailmarkers

✔ Not only does the Bible *contain* figures of speech, one of its descriptions of itself *uses* a figure of speech for that description! Read Hebrews 4:12. What is the Bible compared to? What affect does it have on its listeners?

Teamwork

The chart below contains several passages of Scripture that touch on the subject of money. Identify what kind of literature each passage is, and fill in the appropriate description.

	Passage	Type of Literature
A	Lazy hands make a man poor, but diligent hands bring wealth.	
B	Whoever loves money never has money enough; whoever loves wealth is never satisfied with his income. This too is meaningless. As goods increase, so do those who consume them. And what benefit are they to the owner except to feast his eyes on them? The sleep of a laborer is sweet, whether he eats little or much, but the abundance of a rich man permits him no sleep.	
C	"The ground of a certain rich man produced a good crop. He thought to himself, 'What shall I do? I have no place to store my crops.' Then he said, 'This is what I'll do. I will tear down my barns and build bigger ones, and there I will store all my grain and my goods. And I'll say to myself, 'You have plenty of good things laid up for many years. Take life easy; eat, drink and be merry. But God said to him, 'You fool! This very night your life will be demanded from you. Then who will get what you have prepared for yourself?' This is how it will be with anyone who stores up things for himself but is not rich toward God."	

D	But godliness with contentment is great gain. For we brought nothing into the world, and we can take nothing out of it. But if we have food and clothing, we will be content with that. People who want to get rich fall into temptation and a trap and into many foolish and harmful desires that plunge men into ruin and destruction. For the love of money is a root of all kinds of evil. Some people, eager for money, have wandered from the faith and pierced themselves with many griefs.	
E	All the believers were one in heart and mind. No one claimed that any of his possessions was his own, but they shared every thing they had. With great power the apostles continued to testify to the resurrection of the Lord Jesus, and much grace was upon them all. There were no needy persons among them. For from time to time those who owned lands or houses sold them, brought the money from the sales and put it at the apostles' feet, and it was distributed to anyone as he had need. Joseph, a Levite from Cyprus, whom the apostles called Barnabas (which means Son of Encouragement), sold a field he owned and brought the money and put it at the apostles' feet. Now a man named Ananias, together with his wife Sapphira, also sold a piece of property. With his wife's full knowledge he kept back part of the money for himself, but brought the rest and put it at the apostles' feet. Then Peter said, "Ananias, how is it that Satan has so filled your heart that you have lied to the Holy Spirit and have kept for yourself some of the money you received for the land? Didn't it belong to you before it was sold? And after it was sold, wasn't the money at your disposal? What made you think of doing such a thing? You have not lied to men but to God." When Ananias heard this, he fell down and died. And great fear seized all who heard what had happened.	

| F | "They will say, 'The fruit you longed for is gone from you. All your riches and splendor have vanished, never to be recovered.' The merchants who sold these things and gained their wealth from her will stand far off, terrified at her torment. They will weep and mourn and cry out:
'Woe! Woe, O great city,
dressed in fine linen, purple and scarlet,
and glittering with gold, precious stones and pearls!
In one hour such great wealth has been brought to ruin!'" | |

Reaching the Summit

Write down as many kinds of figures of speech as you can remember from this lesson.

✓ How would you put in one sentence what you are personally going to take away from the discussion?

"It is the task of a reverent interpretation to discover what these figures [of speech mean] both by a comparison of Scripture with Scripture and, not least, by the use of common sense enlightened by the Holy Spirit."
(J. Stafford Wright, *Interpreting the Bible*)

Next Session

Think of a time when you misunderstood some instructions either when building something or when using an appliance, tool or vehicle. Come ready to share the incident with the group.

Close in Prayer

Thank God for language, the ability to put into words what we think and feel. Thank him for putting into language his thoughts and feelings, which we can read in the Bible. Thank him that his rich diversity—and the diversity he wired into us—is reflected in the many forms of literature contained in his Word.

Session 4

Avoiding Interpretation Pitfalls

Identifying frequent reasons people make bad interpretations so you can be more confident you're making good ones.

Establishing Base Camp

Several years ago, a satire magazine published a fictional story about a town meeting where people were trying to come to a joint understanding of a street sign that read, "No Parking After Two-Inch Snowfall." The town was in an uproar because everyone had their own interpretation of what it meant. Questions abounded, such as:

Does the "no parking" apply only in the case of *exactly* two inches of snow? What about 1.9 inches? 1.8? What if there is two *feet* of snow?

How much time must elapse after a two-inch snowfall before you can park again? an hour? a day? a month? Can you *ever* park in the city again?

What if some parts of the city receive less than two inches and parts receive more? Is there a ban throughout the whole city or just the parts with a full two inches?

Which particular vehicles are prohibited? Can you park trucks but not cars? How about boats?

What if you want to park in your driveway (the sign doesn't say where you can't park)?

Does the word *after* mean "in the manner of"? If that is so, is the prohibition really against "parking in the manner of snow falling"; that is, are you not allowed to park your car vertically, dropping it down out of the sky?

Not only were the people confused, they were angry. Why didn't the author of the sign say what he really meant? The meeting ended in deadlock with no one sure what the sign really prohibited.

That story may make us chuckle at how a simple string of words can be interpreted in so many ways, but what happens when we turn our attention to the hundreds of thousands of words in the Bible? How can we avoid some of the common pitfalls of interpretation so we don't get confused or come up with erroneous applications to our lives?

✓ Describe a situation when you misunderstood instructions for building or using something. Was it more the fault of the instruction writer or the instruction reader?

Mapping the Trail

✓ Have you ever been confused by a verse of Scripture? Quote it if you can.

✓ What makes the passage hard to interpret?

✓ Have you ever had a friendly (or heated) argument with someone when the two of you couldn't seem to agree on the meaning of a passage from the Bible? How did the situation end?

Beginning the Ascent

Someone once defined a "cult" as a group organized around some person's misunderstanding of the Scripture. But you don't have to be in a cult to go astray. Either through our own Bible reading or (usually) through something a teacher writes or says, any one of us can be persuaded the Bible means something it actually doesn't. One of the best ways to avoid such a spiritual detour is to know common interpretation pitfalls so you are aware when they happen.

Read through the descriptions of each of the following pitfalls. As a group, discuss those you may have fallen into. Are there other pitfalls you'd add to this list?

Pitfall one: Verses that "jump out" at you. Certainly we should be grateful when God takes a portion of his Word and through the Holy Spirit makes it hit home. Yet sometimes verses stand out that really aren't saying what we think they are. Anytime a verse seems to come at you as if it has a neon sign behind it, check to make sure the context supports what you think God is saying.

Pitfall two: Letting the Bible randomly fall open for guidance. Occult fortune-tellers usually use some tool that generates random words or pictures (Tarot cards, tea leaves, astrological charts and so on) which are then "interpreted." Yet sometimes Christians handle their Bibles like they're fortune-telling! They ask God for guidance and then flip it open, hoping God will speak to them. While this may yield a verse helpful to our situation, it ought never to be used as a normal means for guidance. Think of what would happen if you asked God to lead you, and your Bible fell open to the verse "Judas went out and hanged himself," followed by "Go and do likewise" and ending with "What you do, do quickly"!

Pitfall three: Spiritual or subjective interpretations. Sometimes when discussing a passage, we say, "What that verse means to me is . . . " Someone may well respond, "Is what the verse says to you the same thing the author meant it to say?" If not, the interpretation should be discarded. In extreme cases, words are deliberately redefined so that the verse means something else. Mary Baker Eddy of Christian Science actually has a glossary of redefined words in her *Science and Health with Key to the Scriptures.* By substituting her meanings, the Bible ends up teaching completely different things than what the words meant when written. (The Mormons also do this when they take the word *exaltation* to mean "the progress of a man to godhood," a concept nowhere found in the Bible.) Even if the redefinition is unintentional, we must always be careful not to spiritualize a text meant to be taken at face value or personalize a text not meant for us alone.

Pitfall four: Making a verse contradict other clear biblical teaching. Sometimes a verse can make a claim that seems straightforward enough. Yet when we factor in other passages and get a fuller picture, we must modify our understanding of the isolated verse. A typical example of this is when Jesus says in John 14:14, "Ask me anything in my Name and I will do it." If that were the only teaching in the Bible about prayer, we would assume God has given us carte blanche to make demands on him. Presumably a criminal could ask Jesus for success in his illegal activity; based on this verse alone, he should expect a positive answer. But this interpretation leaves out other teaching on the subject of prayer, which includes several conditions (see for example, James 1:6–7; 4:3; 1 John 3:22; 5:14–15), not to mention the Bible's teaching about how people's hearts are often at odds with God's purposes, and how God's sovereignty includes his absolute right to answer any prayer according to his wisdom on the matter.

Pitfall five: The hapax hazard. Occasionally we come across a verse that teaches something that cannot be corroborated anywhere else in Scripture. Such a verse is a "hapax" (which means "once") and should never be used as a basis for doctrine. An example of this is in 1 Corinthians 15:29, where Paul mentions people being "baptized for the dead." Mormons have constructed an elaborate system of proxy baptism whereby living people are baptized on behalf of dead people. Not only do we not know what Paul was talking about (scholars have assorted theories) but a ritual that somehow saves someone else flies in the face of all the Bible's teaching about personal responsibility. This could all be avoided by never basing any practice or belief on a hapax.

Pitfall six: Forcing verses into interpretive grids. Creative teachers sometimes come up with interpretive filters that screen out some verses and spotlight others—all to the eventual reworking of the meaning of the text. For example, Hebrews 13:8 teaches Jesus Christ is the same yesterday, today and forever. Does that mean every verse in the Bible is equaling binding on all people at all times? Should we go back to animal sacrifices because "Jesus never changes"? If that's what God commanded then (and he never changes), is that what he expects now? Should millions of Christians confidently expect to raise people from the dead because that's what Jesus did? Clearly we need more information beyond saying "Jesus never changes." That phrase alone is a poor interpretive filter and leads to faulty applications (although the verse teaches truly he *is* trustworthy and *doesn't* change).

Another example is when people devise elaborate systems of theology, and then try to rework verses that disagree with that system. Thus Jehovah's Witnesses teach that most of the Bible is addressed to an elite "heavenly class" of believers, therefore, according to them, promises that look like they pertain to average Christians actually don't. By forcing this grid over the Bible, vast portions that were intended for our comfort and edification are removed as irrelevant. They do the same thing when they claim that Jesus was Michael the archangel, and then reread all of Jesus' claims to deity as merely the claim to be a "god" (but not God).

Pitfall seven: Refusing to seek wise counsel. No matter how educated we are, we all have blind spots. The Holy Spirit is our ultimate teacher (1 Corinthians 2:12), but he has structured the body of Christ so that the gift of teaching is distributed among many men and women (1 Corinthians 12:7, 11). Therefore in our ongoing attempts to understand the Bible, we would do well to learn from the great minds God has given the church. C. S. Lewis has suggested that for every book you read by a living author, you should read something by a dead author that has withstood the test of time and is a classic. Also it can be helpful to read things you disagree with to see the faulty logic or exegesis. And it's possible you'll come across something that will change your mind. These are all good exercises that help us develop humility and a teachable spirit concerning God's living and active Word.

Trailmarkers

✓ Read 2 Peter 1:20–21. Who is the real author of the Bible, even though prophets are the mouthpiece? What effect should knowing that have on us as we read the Bible?

> "Pooling of knowledge is edifying to the church; pooling of ignorance is destructive and can manifest the problem of the blind leading the blind." (R. C. Sproul, *Knowing Scripture*)

✓ In Acts 17:11 what caused the Bereans to be called "noble"? Does it seem strange to you that even the apostle Paul had to have his message verified by other Scriptures? Explain.

Teamwork

Using the following verses, compile a profile of false teachers, noting how they mishandle Scripture. For time's sake, you may need to divide into subgroups, assigning a few verses to each team. Then report back on your findings.

Verse	Qualities of False Teachers
Matthew 24:45, 24	
Colossians 2:16-23	
1 Timothy 1:37	
2 Peter 2:13	
2 Peter 3:3-4	
2 John 7-9	

3 John 9-10	
Jude 4, 10, 12, 16, 19	

Reaching the Summit

✓ Have the leader name the first pitfall in this lesson. One person from the group should summarize in a sentence or two that pitfall from memory. Then have the leader read the next pitfall, with another person summarizing from memory. Go around the circle until all the pitfalls have been named and summarized by various members of the group.

Next Session

Can you think of a time in the last week when a principle or verse from the Bible actually influenced—or even redirected—your actions? Come prepared to share an example.

Close in Prayer

Thank God that in the midst of our own ignorance or in spite of teachers who confuse us, we can still know him and move toward clarity about his Word. Ask God to guard you against all the pitfalls discussed in this lesson.

Session 5

What Does the Text Say for Today?

Learning to be a hearer and a doer of the Word.

Establishing Base Camp

She was a new Christian and earnestly wanted to know where to take a nursing job. There were two hospitals in the area—Lutheran General and Mt. Sinai—where she put in applications. She had just finished her schooling and was anxious to enter the health-care industry. She looked forward to the personal benefits and career fulfillment, and also to the opportunities for ministry with the lost and hurting (spiritually as well as physically).

She did what most Christians did when faced with a decision: she prayed about it and read her Bible. What principles from God's Word would direct her? Could she get any guidance from this ancient book for life in modern times?

Much to her discouragement, she had trouble knowing where to begin. What was even more confusing, she kept coming across verses that mentioned "God calling out from Mt. Sinai" or some other reference to the mountain where God gave his Ten Commandments. She received offers from both hospitals, so now she had her choice. Her preference was to work at Lutheran General, but she sincerely desired to know what God wanted, because he saw all the unforeseen circumstances and possibilities. With no other clear direction, all the verses about Mt. Sinai led her to believe God was telling her to take the offer from Mt. Sinai Hospital, despite its longer drive time and slightly poorer pay.

✔ What is commendable about this woman's decision-making process? What additional counsel would you give her?

Mapping the Trail

✓ Were you able to identify a time when the Bible influenced or even redirected your actions this past week? Describe that experience.

✓ If you could get any help at all learning to apply the Bible more effectively, what would it be?

✓ Which is harder for you: discerning what the Bible tells you to do, or actually doing what it says? Why do you believe that is so?

Beginning the Ascent

There are three fundamental missteps we can make when we move from studying the Bible to applying it. The first is to take the result of our study and leave it in the abstract. For example, let's say you read that Jesus expects his followers to treat their enemies kindly, and you agree in principle you ought to do so. You wonder if you have any enemies and conclude that right now you can't name any. So you feel confident there's nothing specific you need to do. Yet just an hour later as you're driving in rush-hour traffic, you feel

intense anger at the driver in front who cut you off—so you drive danger-
ously close behind him to send "helpful encouragement" for him to adjust
his driving patterns! It's easy, in the moment, not to make the connection
between what Jesus said and how you're treating this fellow human being
on the road. But isn't that person in effect your "enemy" now? Isn't Jesus
saying that people in his kingdom live counterculturally, being kind where
it isn't expected or warranted?

The second mistake is to think you have to turn
every Bible passage into a "take action now" list.
Imagine, if you're married, that every time you have a
conversation with your spouse, the only thing you ever
discuss is what you're supposed to do differently. How

> "We would rather be ruined than changed." (W. H. Auden)

would you feel about a relationship that consistently regresses into
demands on you? Yet some people suggest that every time you read the
Bible, you need to get a "to do" list from God. Who *wouldn't* avoid daily
Bible reading if that's all that ever came out of it? Of course, the Bible does
make demands of us. But it offers so much more: encouragement, consola-
tion, hope, inspiration, affirmation and even tender words of love from our
heavenly Father. Those are as much its reason for being as the direction it
gives.

The final mistake is failing to realize that making application often is
more of an art than a science. For example, we read Paul telling us to raise
our children "in the training and instruction of the Lord" (Ephesians 6:4).
But how do we do that in our particular family, with our particular children,
at their particular ages? Clearly, different parents
have to apply that command differently—and the
same parents have to make individualized application
to each child. Putting into action the changeless principles from God's Word still involves using our best
judgment and a generous dose of dependency on the
Holy Spirit in order to follow his instruction. We need
to give each other—and ourselves—grace as we seek
to integrate the wealth of Bible truth into our daily
lives.

> • Don't fail to make applications.
> • Don't get overly rigid about making applications.
> • Don't stop learning how to make better applications.

✓ Which of the preceeding three mistakes are you more prone to? What would help you become more balanced in how you personally interact with the Bible?

Gaining a Foothold

Application Questions

Is there a promise to claim?	Is there a behavior to change?
Is there a command to obey?	Is there encouragement to receive?
Is there a sin to confess?	Is there an insight to gain?
Is there an example to follow?	Is there an issue to pray about?
	Is there a reason to worship God?

(from *Friendship with God: Developing Intimacy with God*
by Don Cousins and Judson Poling)

As you answer the questions listed in "Gaining a Foothold" and make your personal application, it can be helpful to phrase your application in such a way that you can know if you've done it or not. If you say, "I need to be more patient," that's hard to measure, but if you say, "I will purposely pick the long lines at the checkout counter this week to train myself to be more patient," you have a clear target to shoot for.

✓ As you look at the application questions, which applications are you most likely to make?

✓ Which questions do you rarely ask yourself?

✓ What questions would you add to the list?

Trailmarkers

Read 2 Timothy 3:14–17.

✓ In verse 16 what four things is the Scripture useful for?

✓ What additional benefit is described in verse 17?

✓ Read James 1:22–25. Put into your own words the point the author is making with the mirror analogy.

Teamwork

Read Romans 15:1–4. As a group, fill in the following chart. Be sure to refer to the "Application Questions" above as you fill in the middle column.

Observations *What does it say?*	Applications *What should we do?*	Accountability *This is what I will do.*

Reaching the Summit

From memory write down as many of the application questions as you can remember.

Application Questions

Next Session

Identify a passage in the Bible that you would like help understanding. If the passage is confusing primarily because of its doctrinal implications, try to find one instead that is more practical (involving day-to-day concerns).

Close in Prayer

Thank God for the ways in which his Word still speaks to us today. Pray for the courage to make appropriate applications and the wisdom to identify what they should be.

Session 6

Putting It All Together

Practicing interpretation methods.

 ### Establishing Base Camp

During my first year of college I met a fellow freshman who quickly became a good friend. We shared an interest in astronomy, and we also had an irreverent sense of humor. I was a young Christian, and he was an open-minded spiritual seeker. As our relationship progressed, the spiritual conversations became more intense, and by the end of the first semester he committed his life to Christ.

He eventually joined a Bible study I led and practically devoured the Scriptures. He had a keen mind and appreciated a wide variety of literature. As he read the Bible, he immediately noticed its various types of literature and styles. That bothered him because if the book was supposed to be from one God, why didn't it sound like one person wrote it?

I tried to explain the dual authorship of Scripture in the best way I could. My friend patiently tried to grasp my fumbling explanations but always seemed poised to discard his trust in the Bible as a merely human book. Any unclear passage, any apparent contradiction, and he would flounder in his faith.

At the end of the school year, we went home to our respective states. He wrote me a letter describing something he had come across in his Bible that confused him terribly. In Genesis 6:3 he read, "Then the LORD said, 'My Spirit will not contend with man forever, for he is mortal; his days will be a hundred and twenty years.'" According to his interpretation, this passage taught that God had put a limit of 120 years on humankind's life span. Yet Noah himself lived a lot longer than that, as did many other people in later chapters. To my friend this was a bona fide contradiction in the Bible. He was right at the brink of rejecting divine inspiration—and his newfound trust in God.

I had never read this text before, so at first it baffled me too. But it didn't take long for me to see that God was not putting a universal constraint on lifespans but was describing how long it would be before the flood came (building an ark and gathering all those animals took time!). So this was not really a contradiction; my friend had simply misinterpreted this verse. This information greatly relieved him and gave him back his trust in the Bible.

Hopefully, after all these lessons it's crystal clear: the Bible needs to be interpreted correctly. Misinterpretations can lead to crises of faith, which can lead to distrust of God. They can also lead to practices or behaviors that are at odds with God's true instruction and may eventually lead to harm or even death, as in the case of those who refuse medical assistance on the basis of erroneous interpretations.

✓ Have you ever embraced an interpretation of something in the Bible that you later rejected as a misinterpretation? If so, what first caused you to think that mistaken view was correct? What brought about your change in belief?

Mapping the Trail

✓ Think back over all you've learned during these sessions. From memory, briefly list as many rules or principles of good interpretation as you can. (You can do this on your own or as a group.)

What We've Learned About Good Interpretation

When you've completed your recollections, look back over the lessons to see if there are any key principles you've left out. Add them to your list above.

Beginning the Ascent

✓ Read 1 Peter 5:5–11. Begin by making observations. Using the "fly on the wall" analogy, listen in on Peter's message to those first-century believers. What is he saying? Put his message in short statements, using your own words. Do not yet make any application to our day or your own situation.

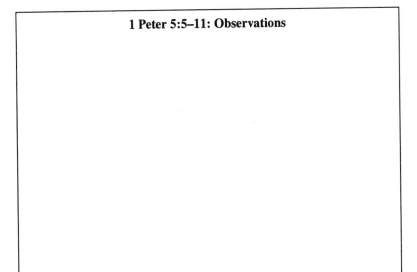

1 Peter 5:5–11: Observations

Some interpretive questions to consider:

✓ *Verse 5:* When you read "in the same way," what or who is referred to?

✓ What do you think the command "be submissive" means?

✓ Isn't it degrading or arbitrary to tell someone to be submissive to a man just because he is older?

✓ What does it mean to "clothe yourselves with humility"? What kind of figure of speech is that?

✓ Peter quotes from another passage at the end of the verse. Where is that from? What kind of literature is it?

✓ *Verse 6:* What does it mean to be "under God's mighty hand"? Does God have a physical body (a hand)? At least two figures of speech are used here—what are they?

✓ What did Peter's listeners think would happen when God "lifted them up"?

✓ *Verse 7:* How could Peter's listeners "cast all their anxiety" on God? What would that look like?

✓ What truth about God is taught at the end of the verse?

✓ *Verse 8:* Were Peter's listeners sleepy? Why were they told to be alert?

✓ What figure of speech is used when Peter compares the devil to a lion? What comparisons are spelled out? What comparisons might be implied?

✓ *Verse 9:* How does someone "stand firm in the faith"?

✓ Who are the "brothers throughout the world"?

✓ Why would Peter remind them of someone else's suffering? What difference would that make? (Compare 4:12 and the following verses.)

✓ *Verse 10:* What does "God of all grace" mean?

✓ How did God "call" them?

✓ How long is "a little while"? Why isn't Peter more specific?

✓ What good would such an ambiguous phrase be?

✓ *Verse 11:* Does Peter think he's giving God power by suggesting "to him be the power for ever and ever"?

✓ If God has power for ever, why does he need power for ever and ever? Is that longer?

✓ What does "amen" mean?

✓ Why is it here?

✓ What's the point of this verse?

✓ Now consider the timeless truths of the passage. What principles are taught which translate into something that is applicable to all God's people, at all times, in all places? List those below. Again, state them in nonpersonal, not-specific-to-you phrases; for example, The experience age brings should generally be respected; or Humility toward God and one another is a fundamental Christian virtue.

---

1 Peter 5:5–11: General Applications

✔ Now conclude with two or three personal applications. Remember: be specific enough that you can know if you've actually done them.

"I can't make the Bible come alive for anyone. The Bible is already alive. It makes me come alive." (R. C. Sproul, *Knowing Scripture*)

1 Peter 5:5–11: Steps I'll Take in Response

Trailmarkers

✓ Psalm 1:1–3 describes a person steeped in the truths of God's Word. What does that person do with God's law (verse 2)?

✓ Those things seem passive; what clues do verses 1 and 3 give as to the kind of applications that are being made?

Reaching the Summit

✓ Summarize how these six sessions have helped you better interpret the Bible. What additional help do you need?

Close in Prayer

Thank God for the light of his Word that blesses us in body, soul and spirit. Pray you will continue to learn more about the Bible, appreciate its wisdom and faithfully live out its priorities.

Leader's Notes

Few ventures are more defining than leading a group that produces changed lives and sharper minds for the cause of Christ. At Willow Creek we have seen small groups transform our church, offer deeper levels of biblical community and provide an environment where truth can be understood and discussed with enthusiasm. So we have focused on a group-based study rather than a classroom-lecture format or individual study (though these studies can profitably be used in both settings with minor adaptations.)

Each method of learning has its strengths; each has its weaknesses. In personal study one can spend as little or as much time on an issue and can focus specifically on personal needs and goals. The downside: there is no accountability to others, no one to challenge thoughts or assumptions, no one to provide support when life comes tumbling down around you. The classroom is ideal for proclaiming truth to many at one time and for having questions answered by those with expertise or knowledge in a subject area. But the pace of the class depends largely on the teacher, and there is limited time to engage in the discussion of personal issues. The small group is optimal for life-on-life encouragement, prayer and challenge. And it provides a place where learning is enhanced through the disciplines of biblical community. But small groups are usually not taught by content experts and cannot focus solely on one person's needs.

Our hope is that you will be able to use this curriculum in a way that draws from the best of all three methods. Using the small group as a central gathering place, personal preparation and study will allow you to focus on your own learning and growth goals. The small group activity will provide you with an engaging environment for refining your understanding and gaining perspective into the lives and needs of others. And perhaps by inviting a knowledgeable outsider to the group (or a cluster of small groups at a Saturday seminar, for example) you could gain the benefits of solid teaching in a given subject area. In any case your devotion to

Christ, your commitment to your local church and your obedience to the Word of God are of utmost importance to us. Our desire is to see you "grow in the grace and knowledge of the Lord Jesus Christ."

Leadership Tips

Here are some basic guidelines for leaders. For more extensive leadership support and training we recommend that you consult *The Willow Creek Guide to Leading Lifechanging Small Groups,* where you will find many suggestions for leading creative groups.

Using the leader's notes. The questions in the study will not be repeated in the leader's notes. Instead, we have provided comments, clarifications, additional information, leadership tips or group exercises. These will help you guide the discussion and keep the meeting on track.

Shared leadership. When leading a small group remember that your role is to guide the discussion and help draw people into the group process. Don't try to be the expert for everything. Seek to involve others in the leadership process and activities of group life (hosting meetings, leading prayer, serving one another, leading parts of the discussion and so forth).

Preparation. Your work between meetings will determine group effectiveness during meetings. Faithful preparation does not mean that you will control the meeting or that it will move exactly as you planned. Rather, it provides you with a guiding sense of the desired outcomes of the time together so that you can gauge the pace of the meeting and make adjustments along the way. Above all, make sure you are clear about the overall goal of the meeting. Then, even if you get appropriately sidetracked dealing with a personal concern or a discussion of related issues, you can graciously help the group refocus on the goal of the meeting. Also, preparation will allow you to observe how others are engaging with the material. *You should complete the study* before coming to the meeting. You can participate in the group activities at the meeting, but take time to become personally acquainted with the material in case you need to alter the schedule or amount of time on each section.

Purpose. The series is designed to help people understand the Word and be confident in their ability to read, study and live its life-changing truths. Bible 101 is not designed for a group whose primary goal is caregiving or support. That does not mean you will avoid caring for each other, praying for needs or supporting one another through personal crises. It simply means that the *entire* focus of the group is not for these purposes. At the same time, the content should never take precedence over the process of transformation. There will be appropriate times to set the curriculum aside and pray. Or you may want to spend an evening having fun together. Remember, Jesus did not say, "Go therefore into all the world and complete the curriculum." Our focus is to make disciples. The curriculum is a tool, not a master. Use it consistently and with discernment, and your group will be well-served. But be clear about the primary focus of the group as you gather, and remind people every few weeks about the core purpose so that the group does not drift. So even though this is designed for six meetings per study guide, you might take longer if you have a meeting that focuses entirely on prayer or service.

Length of Meeting. We assume that you have about seventy to ninety minutes for this meeting, including prayer and some social time. If you have more or less time, adjust accordingly, especially if you have a task-based group. In that case, since you must complete the task (working on a ministry team or serving your church in some way), you will have to be selective in what you cover unless you can devote at least one hour to the meeting. In the format described below, feel free to play with the time allowed for "Beginning the Ascent," "Trailmarkers" and "Teamwork." We have given general guidelines for time to spend on each section. But depending on the size of group (we recommend about eight members), familiarity with the Bible and other group dynamics, you will have to make adjustments. After a few meetings you should have a good idea of what it will take to accomplish your goals.

Format. We have provided you with a general format. But feel free to provide some creativity or a fresh approach. You can begin with prayer, for example, or skip the "Establishing Base Camp" group opener and dive right into the study. We recommend that you follow the format closely early in the group process. As your group and your leadership skills mature and progress, you should feel increasing freedom to bring your creativity and experience to the meeting format. Here is the framework for the format in each of the guides in this series.

Establishing Base Camp

This orients people to the theme of the meeting and usually involves a group opener or icebreaker. Though not always directly related to the content, it will move people toward the direction for the session. A base camp is the starting point for any mountain journey.

Mapping the Trail

In this component we get clear about where we will go during the meeting. It provides an overview without giving away too much and removing curiosity.

Beginning the Ascent

This is the main portion of the meeting: the climb toward the goal. It is the teaching and discussion portion of the meeting. Here you will find questions and explanatory notes. You will usually find the following two components included.

Pullouts. These provide additional detail, clarification or insight into content or questions that may arise in the participants' minds during the session.

Charts/Maps. Visual learners need more than words on a page. Charts, maps and other visuals combined with the content provide a brief, concise summary of the information and how it relates.

Gaining a Foothold
Along the trail people can drift off course or slip up in their understanding. These footholds are provided for bringing them into focus on core issues and content.

 Trailmarkers

These are key biblical passages or concepts that guide our journey. Participants will be encouraged to memorize or reflect on them for personal growth and for the central biblical basis behind the teaching.

Teamwork
This is a group project, task or activity that builds a sense of community and shared understanding. It will be different for each study guide and for each lesson, depending on the author's design and the purpose of the content covered.

Reaching the Summit
This is the end of the content discussion, allowing members to look back on what they have learned and capture it in a brief statement or idea. This "view from the top" will help them once again focus on the big picture after spending some time on the details.

Balancing caregiving and study/discussion. One of the most difficult things to do in a group, as I alluded to above, is balancing the tension between providing pastoral and mutual care to members and getting through the material. I have been in small groups where needs were ignored to get the work done, and I have been in groups where personal needs were the driving force of the group to the degree that the truth of the Word was rarely discussed. These guides are unique because they are designed to train and teach processes that must take place in order to achieve its purpose. But the group would fail miserably if someone came to a meeting and said, "I was laid off today from my job," and the group said a two-minute prayer and then opened their curriculum. So what do you do? Here are some guidelines.

1. People are the most important component of the group. They have real needs. Communicate your love and concern for people, even if they don't always get all the work done or get sidetracked.

2. When people disclose hurts or problems, address each disclosure with empathy and prayer. If you think more time should devoted to someone, set aside time at the end of the meeting, inviting members to stay for additional prayer or to console the person. Cut the meeting short by ten minutes to accomplish this. Or deal with it right away for ten to fifteen minutes, take a short break, then head into the study.

3. Follow up with people. Even if you can't devote large portions of the meeting time to caregiving, you and others from the group can provide this between meetings over the phone or in other settings. Also learn to leverage your time. For example, if your meeting begins at 7:00 p.m., ask the member in need and perhaps one or two others from the group to come at 6:30 p.m. for sharing and prayer. A person will feel loved, your group will share in the caregiving, and it is not another evening out for people.

4. Assign prayer partners or groups of three to be little communities within the group. Over the phone or on occasional meetings outside the group (before church and so on) they could connect and check in on how life is going.

5. For serious situations, solicit help from others, including pastors or other staff at church. Do not go it alone. Set boundaries for people with serious care needs, letting them know that the group can devote some but not substantial meeting time to support them. "We all know that Dave is burdened by his son's recent illness, so I'd like to spend the first ten minutes tonight to lift him up in prayer and commit to support Dave through this season. Then after our meeting I'd like us to discuss any specific needs you (Dave) might have over the next two to three weeks (such as meals, help with house chores, etc.) and do what we can to help you meet those needs." Something to that effect can keep the group on track but still provide a place to express compassion.

Take time to look at the entire series if you have chosen only one of the guides. Though each can be used as a stand-alone study, there is much to benefit from in the other guides because each covers material essential for a complete overview of how to study and understand the Bible. We designed the guides in series form so that you can complete them in about a year if you meet weekly, even if you take a week off after finishing each guide.

A Word About Leadership

One of your key functions as a small group leader is to be a cheerleader—someone who seeks out signs of spiritual progress in others and makes some noise about it. What have you seen God doing in your group members' lives as a result of this study? Don't assume they've seen that progress—and definitely don't assume they are beyond needing simple words of encouragement. Find ways to point out to people the growth you've seen. Let them know it's happening, and that it's noticeable to you and others.

There aren't a whole lot of places in this world where people's spiritual progress is going to be recognized and celebrated. After all, wouldn't you like to hear someone say somthing like that to you? Your group members feel the same way. You have the power to make a profound impact through a sincere, insightful remark.

Be aware also that some groups get sidetracked by a difficult member or situation that hasn't been confronted. And some individuals could be making significant progress, but they just need a nudge. "Encouragement" is not about just saying "nice" things; it's about offering *words that urge*. It's about giving courage (en-*courage*-ment) to those who lack it.

So, leaders take a risk. Say what needs to be said to encourage your members as they grow in their knowledge of the Bible. Help them not just amass more information, but move toward the goal of becoming fully devoted followers of Jesus Christ. Go ahead; make their day!

Session 1. Principles of Interpretation.
Introduce the Session (1 min.) At the beginning of this session (and all others), read the introduction. Vary how this is done. The first week, you can read it aloud. In later weeks, assign different people from your group to read it. You might also suggest the group members read it silently. Maybe one week you could have it on cue cards or sing it. Be as creative as you can as you begin each meeting—but be sure they understand where the session is heading. Go over the purpose and goal with the group.

Purpose: This session is designed to introduce the need for and practice of good interpretation (hermeneutics).

Far from being an academic exercise, we use interpretation skills every day. Newspapers, work memos and personal correspondence are just a few of the areas in which we attempt to accurately understand the written word. The Bible is one more message to which we must listen carefully so we hear what is actually being said and guard against reading what isn't there into the words.

Goal: To recognize the need for good interpretation and have a basic idea of what is needed for such understanding.

Establishing Base Camp (10 min.) By starting with a story about being misunderstood and following up with personal stories of being misunderstood, you're helping group members identify with the *authors* of the Bible. Most people have trouble "getting outside" of themselves, but it is essential to do that if we are to understand the message of the Bible (and do the work of good interpreters).

Mapping the Trail (10 min.) It will be interesting to see what constitutes grounds for confidence among your group members. It will be helpful to know what steps they usually take to move past their confusion. This will help you know what to stress in this lesson and in the weeks ahead.

Beginning the Ascent (30 min.) Read over this material in the group. Have group members take turns reading, or summarize it in your own words.

The diversity of the Bible has its difficult aspects, but it also contains some positives. Among the things group members might say (or you could add):

• The diversity of Scripture suggests God wants to get through to people in a style they enjoy and appreciate. Humanity is diverse and God values that—he and his works reflect and celebrate it.

• The way in which God reveals himself over time helps people see that God is involved in history and accompanies his people for the long haul.

• We have the joy of a lifetime of discovery as we continue to appreciate the Bible's richness and probe its depths.

• We discover God's "normal" methods for working in the world—slowly, over time, at his pace—and our job is to remain faithful whatever happens.

• The Bible is one more piece of evidence—like creation—of God's genius and creativity.

• The diversity of Scripture safeguards against a cultural bias.

• The way the Bible was put together shows that God is powerful and sovereign.

• The Bible shows God's eternality. He is at work in the universe, and the completion of his grand plan is beyond any one generation or culture. (This keeps every generation from self-centered grandiosity.)

• It goes without saying, God probably has many other reasons we don't even know about!

Stress that whatever else is going on, God certainly is not trying to be confusing by revealing his Word as he has. His main message comes through loud and clear, even though parts of the text may be baffling.

Read "Gaining a Foothold" and make sure people understand this "Golden Rule." It would probably be worth having the group memorize it. Have them pair off, say the line and describe to their partner what it means in their own words, then reverse roles.

Regarding the three rules for interpretation from R. C. Sproul: Centuries ago, some Christian thinkers suggested the Bible might have multiple levels of meaning. Many writers became quite adept at embellishing a text. They could take, for example, a simple parable and see specific messages underlying every little detail. One famous "target" was the parable of the Good Samaritan; one commentator suggested the two coins given to the innkeeper (who represents the church) by the Good Samaritan (who represents Christ) signify the two sacraments of baptism and the Eucharist! Such fanciful suggestions are interesting to read, but the biggest problem is that you cannot discuss the merit of the interpretations because nothing other than pure imagination restrains the multitude of possible meanings. These multilevel interpretations get as creative as the person writing them, but they leave us clueless as to what the Bible author was really thinking at the time of writing. Therefore we don't think they are of value for the serious Bible student. We prefer instead (with all due respect to the more creative interpreters throughout church history) the approach known as the grammatical-historical method.

Trailmarkers (10 min.) Paul made it clear he was writing to people with limited education; the gospel is not just for a well-schooled elite but for everyone. (That fact says nothing against education, only that there's no special intelligence level needed to grasp God's message. Even Jesus spoke often with little children and clearly had an impact on them.)

When Peter chides some people for "distorting" or "twisting" the words of Paul, it implies that there is a "straight" meaning of the text, which is preferred. Coming up with "whatever you feel like" is not allowed according to Peter.

Teamwork (15 min.) Another way to do this exercise is to pick two people before the meeting, tell them what they'll have to do (so they can research their characters and prepare) and have them stage the debate. Pick people you know will be able to "get into it" and argue their point of view convincingly. Humor and exaggeration are certainly a possibility. The clerical elite might say, "We'll burn you at the stake, you heretic!" The Reformers would respond, "Who do you think you are, sitting in your ivory tower, throwing God's people crumbs instead of feeding them God's Word?" Just make sure the main points come through.

Reaching the Summit (5 min.) If someone says, "Well, what that verse says to me is . . . " caution the person against reading into the Bible what isn't really there. If the person means "My best understanding of this passage is . . . " that's a good thing. But if the person means "What message I get, regardless of what the author meant, is . . . " that's a problem. We first need to ask what the Bible meant to its original audience. Without that prior step, saying "what it means to me" is very subjective and even dangerous.

Next Session (1 min.) Be sure you, the leader, come prepared with a story next week so you can start things off if group members forget or don't have a good one.

Close in Prayer (8 min.) We suggest you handle this final prayer differently each week. On the first week, you may want to lead the group; in the weeks to come, assign different people to lead or have everyone join in. Sometimes have members get in pairs, sometimes in threes, sometimes pray all together. This is an easy place to customize; be creative each session. If you have an apprentice leader in training, this is a good lesson to assign that person to handle every week. Give that person ideas if he or she needs them, and don't forget to encourage and commend him or her afterward!

Session 2. Context & Culture.
Introduce the Session. Go over the purpose and goal.

Purpose: The Bible's authors were part of a particular culture and historical setting, and were writing for others in the same context, yet their message is also God's Word for all God's people. To better understand what was written we must first know the original context of the message. Then we can make a more informed application of its timeless truth to our own lives.

Goal: To see the need to understand the original setting and context of the Bible's writings.

Establishing Base Camp (10 min.) Most people can identify with a cultural gap that sometimes interferes with communication in day-to-day life. We must not shy away from the reality that a gap exists between us and the original writers of the Bible. (If you think about it, it exists between us and God: his "culture" in heaven is very different from ours on earth.) To admit this problem doesn't mean we become pessimistic about bridging the gap. It merely gives us clarity about the work we have to do to understand the message that God, through biblical writers, sent us.

Some of the factors that help create understanding between cultures are

• love and patience on the part of both parties
• repetition of key points, trying to say the same thing in a variety of ways
• diligence in listening
• trying to "get into the shoes" of the other person
• giving and taking feedback

It's interesting to realize that these are all things God does for us in the process of revelation and illumination.

Mapping the Trail (10 min.) You are probably not going to resolve these questions at this point in the lesson. It's okay to let some loose ends dangle; it will create greater interest and involvement. (By the end of the session and the guide people should have a better handle on these issues.)

Beginning the Ascent (30 min.) Read this section or summarize it in your own words. When you get to the verses, look them up only *after* you've read the excerpt in the lesson. If you read them in context, you'll spoil the point of first seeing them cited out of context.

Note on 1 Corinthians 8:5: the verse is clearly talking about the many "false gods" and "pseudo-lords" of paganism. Paul certainly did not believe there was more than one God, so for him to relegate Jesus to a lesser-god status (as the Jehovah's Witnesses twist this verse to mean) would have been unthinkable. The New Testament writers saw that Jesus is somehow essentially linked to the Father, not as a subgod but as one with the only true God.

Note on Philippians 2:12: Paul did not teach that we work *for* our salvation; he wrote that we need to work *out* (that is, manifest externally) what God graciously works *in* us invisibly through the Spirit. As verse 13 teaches that God is at work in us, surely Paul affirms that salvation is a gift, not the result of human effort. And the "fear and trembling" is a matter of serious intent; based on everything else Paul says about joy, he certainly didn't fear that he wasn't saved.

Note on Ephesians 2:8–10: Paul gives a good summary of the order of spiritual experience: assurance of salvation (versus 8–9), followed by God-assisted good works (verse 10). Self-styled religion typically reverses the order: do good works and then God might accept you.

Note on Galatians 5:1: One possible application for today is in the area of superstition. People often do things "just to be sure," but those practices invalidate trust in God. There are also those who add things to the gospel to try to make it a combination package: God will do something, but you have to do something too or you're not "in."

Note on example one: Clearly Jesus' enemies' animosity toward him contributed to their misunderstanding of what he said. It's hard to hate someone and listen sympathetically!

Note on example two: People slandered Paul by saying his message was a license for sin; even worse, they argued, if God's grace is shown through forgiveness, we ought to sin more so God has more to forgive us for and thus he gets even more glory! Such illogic concerning Paul's message of salvation by grace was a twisting of his teaching. Paul *was* admitting there is a certain "scandalous" nature to the truth that God "justifies the wicked" (Romans 4:5). The false teachers' mindset was that God ought to justify the godly. But no such people exist. All God has to work with are sinners; if they're not the ones he saves, there's no one else available.

Trailmarkers (10 min.) 2 Timothy 2:15: it is not enough just to have the word of truth; it must be "correctly handled," as Paul taught. That is precisely what this lesson and study guide are about. When we do the work of good interpreters, paying attention to context and culture, we're doing what Paul wanted.

Teamwork (15 min.) This may be a good project for someone in your group who likes to do research. This person could present a short report about Bible customs. Whether you assign it or not, try to find some pictures of biblical dress and photos of archaeological sites—any visual support you can find for the culture differences between the Bible and now.

Reaching the Summit (5 min.) You can do this fill-in exercise individually or have people pair off to do it. While they're paired off, have them answer the final question about the one or two tips they'll use in their personal study of the Bible.

Close in Prayer (10 min.) Vary how you do this closing prayer from week to week. See the first session's leader's notes for some suggestions. Are you developing an apprentice leader? This is a good place to give that person some leadership. Remember: the saying that "there is no success without a successor" holds true for small group leadership just as in any other area of life.

Session 3. Discovering the Meaning.
Introduce the Session. Go over the purpose and goal.

Purpose: To discover how to benefit from reading the Bible by finding the meaning of the text rather than reading our own interpretations into it.

"All Scripture is God-breathed," Paul says in 2 Timothy 3:16, but if we misunderstand the message, we're left with an uninspired interpretation. In this day of subjectivism, we rush to talk about what something "means to me." Instead we need to adopt careful study habits and let the Bible speak for itself. That way, we won't invalidate God's timeless truths by putting our personal spin on the message.

Goal: To understand the need for "leading the meaning out of" rather than "reading a meaning into" the Bible.

Establishing Base Camp (10 min.) People in your group may answer this question on either end of the continuum. Some may say that of course it's wrong to misinterpret the Bible, regardless of motives. But others may counter that we're all a little confused about something, yet God doesn't strike us down.

The follow-up question should lead to some interesting discussion because in the short run God doesn't always step in to correct people who are misinterpreting the Bible (Consider the millions of people in cultic groups who do just that.) Yet at some point violation of the principles contained in the Bible does lead to undesirable consequences. Keep in mind that it's okay during these opening questions to leave the issue unresolved as a way to pique interest in the subject of the session.

Mapping the Trail (10 min.) Have several books of different types of literature with you to illustrate this question at the start of the meeting. As you discuss these questions, here are some points to keep in mind:
• Most people appreciate a variety of literature like what we have in the Bible.
• There are advantages to using less direct methods of communication (such as a love poem) because creative use of language can stir the soul at a deeper level and visual language creates pictures that help in understanding and retention. The limitation is, of course, the possibility of misunderstanding. The limitation of plain words is that they might not move the person, and even plain speech can be misinterpreted.

• As far as comparing God's Word to parental communication, it is worth noting that many sections of Scripture do make black-and-white points when that's necessary (such as the "thou shalt nots" of the Ten Commandments); other passages use indirect or subtle means that are effective in their own way.

• God does not want to have the kind of relationship with us where he daily gives us a "to do" list and nothing more. The Bible is not just a series of commandments, because God is not interested in merely being our commander. He wants to be our heavenly Father.

• The Bible contains teaching that is easily grasped by and applicable to a new believer, but it also contains more profound truths that relate to more mature believers. It truly is a "book for life."

Beginning the Ascent (30 min.) Be sure people understand the difference between eisogesis and exegesis. Also stress the point that the usual distinction of taking or not taking the Bible literally is the wrong dividing line. It should be between those who take the Bible for what its authors intended and those who read their own meaning into it.

In addition to what people come up with, you could add

• God's care for us shown in his being described as a mother hen (Matthew 23:37; Psalm 57:1).

• God being secure as a rock and a fortress (Psalm 62:2).

• Jesus our Good Shepherd (John 10:11).

• The church as the body and bride of Christ (1 Corinthians 12:27; Revelation 19:7).

Clearly one of the main reasons people want to change historical events to allegories is because they think those events never happened, but they're not ready to throw out the Bible. Such radical reinterpretation is a shaky compromise between unwillingness to accept the supernatural claims of the Bible and total rejection of it as myth. The problem with such a view is that the Bible writers knew full well their claims were staggering, but they bet their lives on the reality of the events they put their trust in. (1 Corinthians 15:14: "If Christ has not been raised, our preaching is useless and so is your faith.")

As you read through the charts, be sure people have a basic grasp of what each type of literature and figure of speech is. Don't worry that people won't remember each in detail. Just help them grasp the variety presented in the Bible.

Trailmarkers (10 min.) Hebrews 4:12 is a great verse that every believer should memorize. Here the Bible is compared to a sword penetrating deep within our soul. It does not kill, however, like a physical sword. Its effect is closer to the surgeon's knife, which carefully distinguishes between cancerous and healthy tissue, and cuts out disease so healing can occur.

Teamwork (15 min.) Answers: A = Proverb (Proverbs 10:4); B = Poetry (Ecclesiastes 5:10–12); C = Parable (Luke 12:16–21); D = Didactic (1 Timothy 6:6–10); E = Narrative (Acts 4:32–5:5); F = Apocalyptic (Revelation 18:14–17) We suggest you break into smaller groups for this exercise. If people in your group are having trouble, have a cheat card made up which lists the types of literature to choose from. For extra credit, ask who knows the Scripture references without looking them up.

Reaching the Summit (5 min.) First, each member should do this on his or her own from memory. Then have couples or threesomes help each other fill out their lists (without looking back at the pages that list the figures of speech).

Close in Prayer (8 min.) Why not use several styles of literature and figures of speech in your prayer? You will have to do a little preparation, but you could read a poem or a hymn, use visual images, or change your body posture to illustrate your heart—be creative!

Session 4. Avoiding Interpretation Pitfalls.
Introduce the Session. In previous lessons we've learned ways to get at the Bible's message through sound exegesis, accounting for the gap between cultures, and understanding types of literature and figures of speech. Yet there remains the problem of different people coming up with different meanings when reading the same passage.
Go over the purpose and goal with the group.
Purpose: To identify frequent reasons people make bad interpretations, so we can be more confident we're making good ones.
Goal: To be able to identify common interpretive pitfalls.

Establishing Base Camp (10 min.) Although it is true that written communication can often be unclear, this session focuses on how we can strive to be better interpreters. Even if a message is not as straightforward as we'd like, there are steps we can take to get at the truth underlying the words—specifically by avoiding common pitfalls.

When people describe instructions that were misunderstood, you will undoubtedly hear about construction or user manuals that were confusing. Focus, however, on ways people can take even poorly worded documents and get past the clumsy language.

For example, if you were confused about how to put together a product you just bought, one simple step is to go slowly rather than rushing through a manual. Another step is to keep comparing the information presented with the actual pieces you have in your hands for clues to what is meant. A further idea is that when you get stuck, read ahead to see if additional directions or descriptions clarify what is confusing about the step you're on. You might also talk to another user to see what that person's experience can add. And don't forget that you can also set the manual aside for a time and come back to it later; the change in perspective can sometimes help you get clarity. (All of these of course have parallels to what we can do with the Bible.)

Mapping the Trail (10 min.) Do *not* try to resolve the doctrinal or other issues that are presented as people answer these questions. Just talk about the process that happened—good and bad—in the midst of the events people share.

Beginning the Ascent (30 min.) One way to handle this section of the session is to assign each person one of these pitfalls. Have everyone spend a few minutes familiarizing themselves with the pitfall they were assigned; and then one by one have them explain that pitfall to the group. Obviously, depending on how many you have in your group, you may have to double up or assign more than one pitfall per person (there are seven total).

As you go through these pitfalls, try to add some examples of your own. You should be prepared, but first try to draw out the others with examples they think of on the spot. (This would be good preparation to assign your apprentice leader.)

Trailmarkers (10 min.) The verse in 2 Peter is a great description of how inspiration works. The Holy Spirit worked through the authors so that even though it was their words being spoken, they were not the originators of the message. The biblical writers were stirred-up by God, yet he didn't stop there; the Spirit continued to guide through the whole process of speaking and writing. In the words of the apostle Peter, the writers weren't just prodded into writing but were "carried along" by the Holy Spirit.

An interesting parallel to Acts 17:11 is Galatians 1:8-9. There Paul says that neither he nor an angel have the authority to tamper with the gospel message. Imagine that some night an angel came to you and spoke. Paul says here that if you heard a message different from the one Paul preached (as found in his writings), you should reject the angel's message! Clearly, the highest authority is not an angel or even Paul (because he says in verse 8 to reject *him* if he changes his message!). The highest authority is the gospel itself. And that message is in the Bible.

Teamwork (15 min.) As mentioned in the notes, divide into subgroups to do this activity. The reporting back should be a *very* brief summary (a sentence or two).

Reaching the Summit (5 min.) If you had individuals report on a pitfall as part of the lesson, when you do this summary, don't let the group "expert" report on that pitfall.

Make sure a person different from the one who summarized earlier summarizes here.

Next Session (3 min.) Come prepared next week with an example from your own life. Or better yet, have your apprentice leader do this.

Close in Prayer (10 min.) You might have everyone stay together and encourage people to pray very short, one-phrase or one-sentence prayers. They can all pray multiple times during the prayer time, but experiment with these short, "staccato" prayers.

Session 5. What Does the Text Say for Today?
Introduce the Session (5 min.) Once you've correctly understood a passage of Scripture, you still must ask, "What is God telling *me* to do?" It is possible to get the meaning right but make a poor application—or no application at all. Go over the purpose and goal with the group.

Purpose: To make good applications that will help us to be doers of the Word and not just hearers.

Goal: To understand simple ways to apply the Bible's teaching to today's living.

 Establishing Base Camp (10 min.) We certainly can commend the woman in the opening story for her earnest desire to do God's will and her willingness to let him direct her even against her preferences. But frankly, she was not reading the Bible's message, because although she had the pages of her Bible open, she was not at any point actually responding to the meaning the original author intended. She was using an occult technique called "divination," using words (not the message) from the pages of her Bible. Her misuse of the Bible could have led to far worse consequences and is a poor method for getting guidance from the Holy Spirit.

Mapping the Trail (10 min.) Be sure you or your apprentice leader have an example to share of how the Bible actually influenced an action.

On the last question, group members will probably say that it is harder to obey the Word than to understand it. Whatever confusion may attend some parts of the Bible, clear messages are often difficult to implement because we are sinful. Deep in our souls, the dark truth is that we are in rebellion against God and don't *want* to obey.

Beginning the Ascent (30 min.) Be sure to encourage people to be honest about the kind of mistakes they make when they apply the Bible. This openness will serve them as they try to make changes in the future. Here again, as group members talk about what kind of applications they're more likely or less likely to make, try to be ruthlessly honest about what holds them back from a more balanced approach to application.

Trailmarkers (10 min.) Someone once described the steps in 2 Timothy

3:16 as parallel to learning to drive a car. First there is instruction, the basics of how to do it. Then when you make a mistake, there is a quick rebuke that gets you out of danger. That's followed by correction—how to do it right the next time. Training follows—repetition of the correct procedures, feedback and further practice. God's Word, like a good driving instructor, offers us all this.

Note on James 1:22–25: Let's say some morning you look at yourself in the mirror and notice your hair needs combing. Yet when you walk away, you can't see yourself anymore, so after you finish getting dressed, you don't bother combing your hair. How do you look at that point? On a spiritual level, when God's Word points out some need in our life, but we just ignore the change, we look like the well-dressed person with serious "bed head." We're a spiritually well-dressed but disheveled person left in that state because we've failed to act on what we learned about ourselves from the mirror of God's Word.

Teamwork (15 min.) This is by no means exhaustive but will give you some ideas for what could be in each of the columns. Why not have your apprentice leader come to the meeting already prepared with some ideas for each of these columns?

Observations *What does it say?*	*Applications* *What should we do?*	*Accountability* *This is what I will do.*
1. Stronger people ought to be patient with those who aren't so strong. 2. We should be concerned for other's well-being. 3. Christ is a good example of someone who put others first; he was willing to take upon himself the insults aimed at God. 4. The Scriptures apply to us and will give us hope so we can endure and be encouraged.	1. Find ways to help those who are weaker. 2. Find ways to help those around us. 3. Take courage from Christ's example. 4. Spend time in the Word so we can be encouraged and have greater hope.	1. Count to ten when my daughter tries my patience this week. 2. Write a note of encouragement to Jim at work by Thursday. 3. Write the phrase "Christ did not please himself" on a 3x5 card and keep it on my car's visor this week to remind myself to do the same. 4. Schedule three times to be alone with God and read the Bible this week.

Reaching the Summit (5 min.) Each person should do this alone. Then see how the group members did.

Close in Prayer (10 min.) For variety, pray in pairs this week. We suggest the people pair up with someone they're not usually with. (For example, if you have couples, make sure spouses are with group members other than their spouses; if people tend to sit together with close friends, have the group mix it up more.)

Session 6. Putting It All Together.

Introduce the Session. The Bible is a full library of books that offers a lifetime of rewarding study. Yet it is also a guidebook for life and needs to be regularly assimilated and obeyed. These past five sessions have attempted to help us make better interpretations as we read and study the Bible. Proper interpretation leads to right belief and paves the way for appropriate action. With the group, go over the purpose and goal for this session.

Purpose: To practice some of the interpretive methods we've discussed in this guide.

Goal: To practice together making good interpretations of a selected text.

Establishing Base Camp (10 min.) Before the session, assign your apprentice leader (or someone in the group) to come prepared with an example from his or her life in case others are slow to join in.

Mapping the Trail (10 min.) As the session notes describe, you can do this individually or together.

Beginning the Ascent (30 min.) Depending on how much time you have, let group members share the passages they thought of during the week that they would like help understanding. Pick one of them and have everyone discuss what is a good interpretation of that passage. Don't be discouraged if you can't resolve the matter in this meeting. At least identify what issues remain. (Is there a cultural statement? a figure of speech? a confusing context? an apparent contradiction? a grid the verse doesn't fit into?)

You will not have time to do a detailed exegesis of this whole passage. We include all the interpretive questions so your group members can see the types of questions that are useful to try to answer. Before the lesson you may want to assign someone in the group to do a little study using a commentary or other Bible study aid. That person can have some thoughts written down that attempt to answer the interpretive questions posed. For time sake, you may find it helpful to subdivide the group to come up with observations.

When you move on to the "General Applications" box, see how far people got in the observation section. Don't worry if they didn't finish the whole passage. Make applications only on verses where observations were made. (It wouldn't make sense to apply something you didn't have time to observe!) Again we recommend you, your apprentice leader or someone in the group come prepared with ideas for this section.

When you get to the "Steps I'll Take in Response" box, have everyone make at least one specific application. If everybody only has one, that's okay; don't worry about too many specific action steps. Better one resolution carried out than a hundred unfulfilled good intentions—it's unrealistic to think people are going to do much more than one or two things in response to this study.

Here's another option for how to handle this session: If your group members are open to it, have them do homework before the session and come with the three boxes ("Observations," "General Applications" and "Steps I'll Take in Response") already filled out by time you meet. Then the meeting will be a discussion of a passage they've already studied. You can still discuss one other passage at the end; that work would be done without advance preparation. The advantage to doing the work on 1 Peter 5 before the meeting is that the discussion will probably be a lot deeper; the disadvantage is that everyone might not have time to do the work before the meeting, and those people would feel left out.

When you discuss the problem passage the group votes on at the end, keep in mind you don't have to tie up all the loose ends. As a leader, you're training people in a process, and it's how you go about interpreting the passage, not whether you get to a completely satisfying solution at this time. If people are trained on the right kinds of questions to ask and the right process to follow, it will do more for them in the long run than having you be a "Bible answer expert" and resolve all their confusion in this one short session.

Trailmarkers (10 min.) If you can come with an actual picture of a tree by a river, it will help people visualize the message of this verse as you discuss it. (Any time you can bring a visual aid, it helps the learning process because most learning is visual, even for people with verbal or active learning styles.)

Reaching the Summit (5 min.) We suggest you not subdivide the group; do this summary together as a way to cement the group experience at the close of this study.

Close in Prayer (10 min.) Stay in a large group for your prayer time. Since this is the last meeting of this study, you may want to have a slightly longer meeting to allow for more prayer time together.